The Editor wishes to thank the following for their gene

Francis Bernhardi
Carlo and Lynda Bernhardi
Scott and Thomas Bernhardi
ASE Consulting
Roger Baker
Barclays Bank plc (Charnwood Group)
Alison Bowles
Michael Brewer
Candis Club
Jeanne Carswell
Coalville Publishing Company Ltd.
Tracy Cox
Steve Duckworth
Lawrence Grady
Audrey and Graham Hamilton
Rita Hankey
Doreen Hill
Carol Hillyard
Sue Hollins
Josie Hutchinson
Robert Leaf
Leicester Circuits Ltd.
Leicester Library (Humanities Dept)
Mr Duncan McNeil
Leicester Mercury
Joan Manuel
Mr Hasmukh Jivan Mistry
Ann and David Mitchell
Gerry Moon
Valerie Moore
Hazel Morley
Maz of Photo Centre
Ray and Ruby Pannell
Alex and Helen Patterson
Graham Patterson
Steven Peace
Redwood Books
Saga Magazine
St Margaret's Co-operative Bowling Club
Pat and Orville Singer
Janet Stevenson
Mrs Barbara Tom
Mark Wilde
Joyce Woodley
Zahn Dental Supplies Ltd.

To Carlo

FIRST MEMORIES

OF THE

FAMOUS

Compiled and edited by
JILL BERNHARDI

Illustrated by MARK WILDE

Coalville Publishing Company Ltd.

Typesetting by Steve Duckworth
Design by Jill Bernhardi and Steve Duckworth

Printed by Redwood Books, London & Trowbridge

ISBN No. 1 872479 19 7

CANCER RELIEF

Macmillan

FUND

Fighting cancer with more than medicine

Registered Charity Number 261017

Dear Reader

It is only through the tremendous generosity and support of people like yourself, that Cancer Relief Macmillan Fund has been able to carry on the fight against cancer.

With over 6,000 new cases of cancer being diagnosed in the United Kingdom every week, the demand for Macmillan specialist cancer services is increasing relentlessly.

Every penny from the sale of this charming book goes directly to fund the work of Macmillan nurses and other Macmillan cancer care services for people living with cancer near you.

Enjoy reading, as I have, these beautiful memories, some comic, some tragic, but all somehow very touching coming from such celebrated contributors.

Thank you for helping us help others live with cancer.

Susan Zetland

The Marchioness of Zetland

President

The Contributors — who have given so generously of their time and thought.

The Editor would like to thank:-

Jane Asher
Jasper Carrot
The Carter Centre, Atlanta
The Chief Rabbi
Joan Collins
The Earl of Lichfield
Paul McCartney
Virginia McKenna
President Ronald Reagan
Lady Redgrave
Griff Rhys Jones
Sir James Savile
Delia Smith

All of whom sent their best wishes.

FIRST MEMORIES
OF
FIVE GENERATIONS

I have been fascinated by first memories ever since my grandmother told me hers. In 1873 aged 2 she suffered a bad fall. The doctor was called to the Aberdeenshire farmhouse and he placed two leeches on the child's bruised and swollen forehead to suck out the bad blood. My grandmother always remembered looking up and seeing the black creatures at work just above her eye.

My mother's earliest memory was of watching the funeral procession of King Edward VII in London, 1910.

My own first memory was during a family visit to Aberdeen in 1938. Watching a counter-marching Highland pipe band and, each time they advanced, terrified that the Pipe Major was coming to steal my ice cream!

My son's earliest memory is of our house in Australia in 1971, its long driveway and gum trees.

My grandsons, aged 6 and 3, when asked their earliest memory replied "Eating chocolate pudding at Grandma's today."

Jill Bernhardi

JILL BERNHARDI

MY EARLIEST MEMORY

Lying on the grass on the side of a hill in
the Wicklow Mountains in Ireland awaiting the
lighting of a great bonfire in honour of my
father's return from the South African war.
I must have been about four years old.

Ninette de Valois

Dame Ninette de Valois

My earliest memory
was looking at the
white lining of the hood
of my pram — snugly
wrapped in an Indian
shawl, whilst being pushed
gently around the Park.
(Hyde Park in London.)

Duncan Russell

FROM THE BISHOP SUFFRAGAN
OF MALMESBURY

Dear Jill,   1.5.96.

        My first childhood memory is of sitting on the edge of a
bay-window 'underhang', having crawled out of my cot onto a window-cill,
then out of the window to drop 3 feet onto the roof of the room below.
Whilst surveying the universe from there I was spotted by an errand
boy who alerted my father. My next image is of him coming out of the
window head first to save me - his waistcoat buttons flying off as he
desperately lunged down. THe image of the flying buttons is still vivid,
as is that of sitting in the bathroom wash-basin shortly afterwards,
wondering what all the fuss was about.

        Another memory (I don't know whether it pre-dates the above)
is of escaping from the pram-straps, crawling to the bottom, tipping it
up and staring at the grass from ground level. And I **still** retain, in
some part of my awareness, the rhythmical sensation of the pram-wheels
vibrating over the paving stones as I was wheeled along - a calming and
satisfying memory.

        So, take your pick. . I hope that the venture is a success,

                Warmest wishes,

                yours sincerely

                Peter Fink.

My earliest memory

I cannot decide which of two images came first.

In one I am in a pram wheeled by my mother in Sefton Park, Liverpool. To amuse me, she is dragging her umbrella along some cast-iron railings.

In the other a maid with fat red arms is hanging up washing in a sooty back garden. There is a sycamore tree and, between the branches a blue sky with small white clouds. I have very little impression of space.

Yours nostalgically George Melly.

Geoff Hamilton • Barnsdale, Oakham, Rutland

My earliest memory does not, I hope, have deep psychological meaning.

Sitting facing my twin brother in a double pram, I delighted in leaning forward and pulling out his hair! We're still good friends.

Geoff Hamilton.

Dear Jill Bernhardi,

"FIRST MEMORIES OF THE FAMOUS"

My first childhood memory is struggling up
a beach of pebbles at Felpham in Sussex
after a swim to reach the haven of an
enveloping towel and a cuddle from my
Mother!

Yours sincerely,

June Whitfield

June Whitfield

Michael Bentine, C.B.E.

My earliest memory is of
looking through the banisters
of the upstairs landing in
our house in Folkestone.
I was gazing, wide-eyed,
at a "robed" and bearded
stranger standing in the
hallway below.
He laughed and
started to come up the stairs.
It was my father, in full
make-up and costume, as
'Peter Quince', the part he
was playing in the Folkestone
Amateur Dramatic Society's

Michael Bentine, C.B.E.

production of "A midsummer
nights' Dream."

As a well-conditioned,
very young, Christian child
I thought it was Someone
else.

I gave a yell:
"Jesus!" I cried, Thinking
He was coming to "get-me!"
and burst into tears.

Sincerely

Michael
Bentine

'Keep up your Splendid work.'

9

Edith Macarthur

Having reached an age when memory begins to play tricks, I'm not sure whether this is in fact the earliest, but it's one of a few picture images I have of myself as a toddler.

I'm swinging on the gate of our house - it's a late summer afternoon about 1930 - and as I look up the path at our kitchen window, I can see my young mother, and my grandmother, who'd come to visit us. As they look out, laughing and waving to me to come in, I wave back but keep swinging, carefully facing them - with good reason. My grandmother was a dressmaker, and had brought me a beautiful little frock she'd made specially for me, and which I was wearing for the first time, having promised faithfully not to dirty or spoil it. But - I'd gone to play with neighbour's children, and CLIMBED A TREE - result, a great tear in the back of the skirt!

In memory, I'm still swinging on the gate, hiding my back. I don't remember the going in, the confession, the revelation, and the concern and hurt to my lovely Granny at the ruin of all her work, and I certainly don't remember punishment.

I must have been forgiven. All other memories of her, and of my mother, are of love.

I expect dresses are not so important after all, are they.

— Edith Macarthur -

My first memories are of moments on my father's back, my mother walking alongside, and being fed lovely red cherries.

With all good wishes,

Yours sincerely,

DAVID KOSSOFF FRSA Hon D Litt

The woman in whose house my parents rented 'the upstairs' was very fat and jolly and simple. She loved peanuts, and kept a supply in her apron, putting the shells in a paper bag hung from her vast waist. She was kindly & ignorant. She liked all children —and gave them nuts. One of her sons was mentally retarded, another became a world-famous jazz pianist. Her daughter took over and ran a large family business. This nuts memory is from my fourth year

David
Kossoff

26/3/94

SUSAN HAMPSHIRE

I remember sitting on platform at the station waiting with my sisters for my mother to return from London. I longed for the (my mother's) smell of her coat & her hair. I was always so happy to see her. Susan Hampshire

FROM THE ANGLICAN ARCHBISHOP OF CAPE TOWN
The Most Reverend Desmond M. Tutu, D.D. F.K.C.

My first memories are of my mother, not very educated but oh so gentle & caring & kind, always ready to be on the side of whoever was having a rough time & so welcoming & generous. I loved the ... her character. ...

HOUSE OF COMMONS
LONDON SW1A 0AA

10 April 1996   From Tony Benn

Dear Jill Bernhardi,

I think my very earliest memory must be of being in a room
where there was a very, very old lady, lying in a bed and I
stood there wondering who she was. She was, in fact, my
grandmother who died when I was three.

Good luck with the book.

With best wishes,

Tony

IAN McSHANE

Earliest Memory:

Being bathed in a tin tub in front of a blazing coal fire, and then wrapped in a big towel at my grandma and grandpa's.

B Conley
c/o Victoria Palace Theatre, London

My First Memories
by Brian Conley - World Famous Actor/Comedian and
Right Clever Dick!

My first memory as a child was being picked on. Every day after school I used to get beaten up. So finally I spoke to my parents about it. I told them straight.

I said "Mum, Dad, stop hitting me".

My second memory was that I came from a very poor family. At Christmas time, if I hadn't been a boy, I would never of had anything to play with!

We were so poor we couldn't afford central heating. So in the evenings we used to sit round a candle, and if it was really cold we used to light it!

Happy Memories,

Best Wishes,

Brian Conley

ALFRED MARKS, O.B.E.

My first memory was 'getting my first laugh'.

I was four years of age when my mother brought home my baby sister from the maternity hospital. On watching my mother change her napkin I cried out, "Hey! The baby 'aint got no whopper!"

Dr. Patrick Moore, CBE, FRAS

My earliest memory goes back to 1926. I was
then aged three.

We lived in Bognor Regis, and at the time of
the General Strike it so happened that Bognor
was a non-union town. I distinctly remember
my mother saying that I needed a new pair of
shoes. So we got into our car - a 1917 Hupmobile - and drove into the town to a shop
named Leonard's, where I duly tried on new
shoes. We then drove home. What happened after
that escapes me ...

That Hupmobile was a great car. It would do
40 mph, and it was very comfortable; the only
problem was that it apparently had no brakes
of any description! I wish we had it now!

Patrick Moore

Hope this will do!

House of Lords

CHILDHOOD MEMORY

I think my most frightening childhood memory of my life was a journey from Weston-super-Mare in Somerset to Leeds in Yorkshire. The purpose of the journey was to visit an Aunt and Uncle who were school teachers in North Allerton and as I had never travelled beyond Bristol or Bridgewater I looked forward to the day with much anticipation and relish. My Grandmother was one of those early drivers who had not required a licence and had she ever taken the test she would have undoubtedly frightened the examiner out of his wits.

We left Weston-super-Mare early in the morning in a large green Morris Oxford. My Grandmother drove, my Grandfather and Mother in the back while I had the honour of sitting in the front, decades before any one had thought of seatbelts. My Grandmother like myself rarely travelled beyond the environs of Weston-super-Mare and for her the roundabout was a new fangled invention which she had not encountered before. We discovered the first one some seven miles outside my home town over which she happily drove straight across the middle and carried on in a northerly direction. We encountered twenty three such obstacles set unnecessarily in our progress, on our route between Weston-super-Mare and Leeds and my Grandmother crossed all of them in a manner which would have pleased Hannibal.

On arrival in Leeds, my Grandfather who had learnt several years before not to speak, my Mother who was not listened to when she did, and I who did not murmur a word, breathed more than a sigh of relief when we eventually arrived at my Uncle's front door in one piece. Once safely on the premises I ventured the innocent question of my Grandmother 'Surely one should go around roundabouts and not across them', to which she replied with British certainty 'Certainly not. What you must understand young man, is that they will never catch on', a degree of logic with which I am quite unable to find fault.

We returned home by train.

March 10, 1994

Dear Ms. Bernhardi,

On behalf of President Nixon below is a response to your request.

"Well curiously enough, my first memory is of running. I recall when I was about three or three and a half years of age that my mother was driving a horse and buggy, a very fast horse. She was carrying my younger brother who was then one, Don, on her lap and a neighbor girl, who was about 12, was holding me. The buggy turned a corner and the horse took off and the neighbor girl dropped me. I fell out of the buggy. I got a crease in my scalp and I jumped up afterwards and I was running, running trying to catch up because I was afraid to be left behind. Incidentally, I had a wound from that for many years there after. I wasn't able to part my hair on the left due to the fact that I had about 15 stitches down that scalp."

This question and others can be answered by the President at the Presidential Forum exhibit here at the Library. Touch-screens enable visitors to ask President Nixon almost 300 questions and see his answers on the big-screen monitor.

Thank you for your interest in President Nixon. If I can be of any other assistance please contact me.

Sincerely,

Kevin Cartwright
Assistant Director

18001 Yorba Linda Boulevard · Yorba Linda · California USA 92686
Telephone: (714) 993-5075 Fax: (714) 528-0544

WOLF MANKOWITZ

Wolf Mankowitz   March 14/96

My first coherent & complete
memory is of being lost (in
the area of Liverpool St
Station) — my mother having
been distracted for a moment —
Wandering among giants —
crying — being picked up by
a huge policeman — being
given a giant slice of bread &
black currant jam at the police
station & being entertained by some
doting women (policewomen?) till
my mother turned up. I was 3.

18th June 1996

Dear Miss Bernhardi,

You asked for some 'first memories'. I have two.

One - the death of my younger brother. He was a twin and had he lived beyond three days he would have been called Kalman. His twin, Gaby, did survive but was in fact put to death at Auschwitz when he was eleven. What I most remember about the death of Kalman, was the gentle way in which members of our Community came into our home, collected him and left with expressions that gave real comfort to those of us who remained behind.

The other memory is the first day at Religion School, which was called **cheder**. I was not quite four years old and the teacher in charge took out a laminated page of Biblical text - put a spoonful of honey on it and asked all of us new boys to lick it. "Does it taste sweet?" he asked. Enthusiastically we said "Yes it did." He then added, "Well, the words of the Torah (Scriptures) also taste sweet and I hope that you will enjoy them for many years to come". And I did and I still do.

With all good wishes

I am, sincerely yours,

Rabbi Hugo Gryn

Communications to be addressed to
33 SEYMOUR PLACE LONDON W1H 6AT
TELEPHONE 0171-723 4404
FAX   0171-224 8258

Senior Rabbi
RABBI HUGO GRYN
Associate Rabbi
RABBI JACQUELINE TABICK
Executive Director
MAURICE ROSS

Registered Charity No. 212143

From: Dame Barbara Cartland, D.B.E., D.St.J.

My earliest memory was when I was
the age of not quite 2. I received
for Christmas what seemed to me to be
an enormous Dolls House from my Grandmother.

Her name was Mrs. James Cartland
and she was a direct descendent of
King Robert The Bruce.

The first memory I had as a child was in South Africa where my family had moved because of World War II. It was 1942 and I was two years old. I was walking in Prime Minister Smuts's garden during a reception for Greek Air Force officers. He was holding my hand. Suddenly a cow broke loose from an adjacent farm and wandered into his flower bed. He let go of my hand and went into the flower bed to chase the cow away with his stick.

This memory is even more strongly imbedded in my mind because many years later the then President De Klerk took me back there and the patio and garden were still as I remembered them. And there were still cows on the adjacent land. I found out that they were there as the result of Cecil Rhodes's wish for cows always to be there to provide milk for the local inhabitants.

Amman
July 1996

The most stirring memories of my early childhood were of the overpowering majesty and force of the Pacific ocean where I lived as a child. I remember being lulled to sleep by the surf and awakening to look upon the open and unlimited horizon connecting my own small world with those of so many other peoples and cultures in the world.

All these years later, and despite having crossed many oceans and seas throughout my life, I am continuously awed by the wonders of our global village and the waters and horizons that link us all.

The Rt Hon Paddy Ashdown MP

HOUSE OF COMMONS
LONDON SW1A 0AA

My first memory, which may well have been much added to by nightmares which I had about it afterwards, was of a time when I must have been aged about four and a half and I was being taken by my mother from the north of India by train to Bombay, where we were to embark on a ship that would take us to the United Kingdom. This was, in effect, the beginning of the end of nearly two hundred years in India for my family.

We had left behind my father who did not return until 1947 and who, being an Indian Army Officer, was involved in the partition between India and Pakistan.

As you may know, the partition was a dreadful and bloody affair. Many millions of people were killed in religious riots. My memory is of the train stopping outside some Indian station. I can remember quite clearly almost sensing the fear amongst my fellow passengers. I can also remember a sickly sweet smell that I did not experience until much later in my life when I was involved in the war in Borneo. After what seemed to be a very long wait, the train slowly pulled through a station which, as my memory recalls it, was covered from end to end with dismembered bodies which had rotted in the heat of the Indian summer. I had dreams about this sight for many years afterwards.

I hope that this is of some interest and that it doesn't frighten people too much to put in your book.

Yours sincerely

Paddy Ashdown MP

JOANNA LUMLEY

My earliest memory: a port in the Middle East, Aden, perhaps, or Port Said; the reflections of water dappling the ceiling of a lofty white-washed room. We were on our way home on leave from India and I must have been a year old - there was the smell of oil from the troopship's engines, and everywhere the great shadowed heat of Central Asia in the Mid-day Sun.

Joanna Lumley

TERENCE CONRAN

My First Memory

I can't have been much more than two years old. My parents moved from Esher — where I was born — to Hampstead when I was three, yet I have one very vivid memory of playing at home in Esher.

I was sitting on the kitchen floor, no doubt under the watchful supervision of my mother. And I accidentally spilt some green paint on the terracotta tiled floor. The memory of the jarring combination of colours is as clear to me today as if it had happened only last week.

Terence Conran
February 1996

HOUSE OF COMMONS
LONDON SW1A 0AA

The Office of the
Leader of The Opposition

My earliest memories are from the years I spent in Australia as a small boy in the 1950s.

I remember travelling in a car, sitting in the back seat carrying my baby sister who had just been born. This is a special memory because I was very close to her.

Another memory I have from around the same time is very different. It is not what I would call a fond memory. I was out walking one day when a collection of Magpies decided to attack me, which was not a particularly pleasant experience. It could have resulted in some very nasty injuries, but I was able to deter them by waving my arms around and shouting at them to "Get off".

Tony Blair

HARRODS LIMITED, KNIGHTSBRIDGE, LONDON SW1X 7XL   TELEPHONE: 0171-730 1234 • TELEX 24319 • FAX: 0171-581 0470 • REGISTERED IN LONDON NO 30209
TELEGRAPHIC ADDRESS - EVERYTHING LONDON SW1

26 March 1996

Dear Miss Bernhardi,

My earliest memory is of seeing a peerless blue sky above a sea that was calm and welcoming. The scene was so enticing that I think I knew that I would have to cross that sea to find my happiness and fulfilment and so it has proved.

Kind regards,

Yours sincerely,

M. Al Fayed
Chairman

a First memory.

It is perhaps as odd as it is unusual that my very first memory gave me a sign or a symbol. I have ~~followed~~ managed to follow all my life.

I was brought up in India and there came a time when my mother was so ill she had to be sent back to England for a while; she took my elder sister John with her leaving me in the charge of my spinster aunt mary and my father who was stationed in gauhati. assam. I was just three.

The memory that flashes brilliantly clear is of walking with aunt mary down a lane of dusty white sand bordered by bushes higher than my head. each covered with small bright red and orange flowers. called in India fever flowers- under an equally bright blue sky. In my hand is a matchbox and in the matchbox a tiny doll sent to me by John from England. The doll is not like any other doll because she is made in one piece but the most curious thing about her is that everytime she is knocked over ~~she stands~~ straight away ~~and by herself~~ she stands up again. I am fascinated.

Of course I know now that her base is weighted with lead but she remains vivid because again and again I have been knocked over flat yet yet mysteriously ~~and by myself~~ have managed to stand up again

Dear Jill Bennardelle.

Will this do? It is true.

all success

Rumer godden

SARAH GREENE

25th April 1996

Dear Jill,

Many thanks for your letter. One of my earliest memories is staring very hard at my father's hands — comparing them to my own and thinking how extremely big, strong, and hairy they looked! I even remember telling myself at the time never to forget this particular moment. I must have been about three years old, very happy and very safe. Good luck with your book.

Very Best Wishes,

Sarah Greene

SIMON BRETT

My first memory comes with photographic back-up. I can see the picture now. The setting was a Cornish beach in the late 1940s and the photograph of course in black and white. By one of those streams which flatten out to little more than a strip of wet sand, stands an ecstatic small boy. He has blond curls and wears a bathing costume that was one of the early experiments in the use of nylon. I remember it as blue, though of course in the picture it's grey. The nylon was quilted with elasticated thread, giving the material the effect of bubble-wrap. It wasn't a flattering garment for a pot-bellied infant.

But sartorial considerations didn't worry the small boy in the photograph. He was me, incidentally, and the cause of my ecstasy was what I held in my hand. It was a tiny fishing rod and line, at the end of which was a hook with a fish attached. The beam on my face showed that no angler was ever prouder of his catch.

Only closer examination reveals one or two oddities about the picture. For a start, the stream in which I'd apparently been fishing was not deep enough to sustain life in one individual piece of plankton. Second, my catch had been hooked, not in the traditional way through the mouth, but through its tail. And third, what I had caught was, unmistakably... a kipper.

The pride in my early piscatorial achievement stayed with me for a long time. Soon after I started at prep school, the conversation turned one day to the subject of fishing, and I nonchalantly announced that I had once caught a kipper. It was only the immediate raucous laughter of my contemporaries that prompted me then to question my parents about an incident which had become part of family mythology.

They came clean pretty quickly. The deed had been done for the best of motives. I'd been so desperate to catch something that my mother had distracted my attention while my father attached the previously-purchased kipper to my hook. Another childhood illusion shattered. Another example of the duplicity of the adult world.

I've forgiven my parents now, mind. I'm even quite proud of what happened. It's not everyone who can say that their first memory is of catching a kipper.

Simon Brett

March 4th 1994.

One of my earliest memories is
being in a pram in York outside a
wet fish shop. Fish, have always
had an irresistible fascination for
me - I imagine this is when it began.
I don't remember actually taking the
kippers - but I do remember the smell
and my Mother recovering them
from my pram !!

Judi Dench.

Age 4½

Catching ~~first~~ first fish
ever, on rod & line
in Grand Junction
Canal. Berkhamsted.
Made to put it back
(too small) by older
brother.

Michael Hordern

MARTI CAINE

I remember rubbing my tongue over my 'pre toothed' gums until they tingled

Marti Caine

WITH COMPLIMENTS

BBC RADIO 2
BROADCASTING HOUSE
LONDON W1A 1AA
TELEPHONE: 071 580 4468
TELEX: 265781
FAX: 071 436 5247

29/12/93

Dear Julie,

My earliest memory was of
being taken to the doctor to
have my tongue SNIPPED. I had a
"tongue tie" and in those days
the doctor cut it with a
pair of SILVER SCISSORS. I guess
I was around 1 year +.

I also seem to remember my
sister pushing me in a dolls
pram when I was a baby.
However, this is not as
clear as the first memory.

Hope your project goes well.

Kindest Regards

Steven.
Humphries
x

43

I remember a summer holiday before I could properly walk, I was still crawling, and I distinctly remember crawling behind some huts on the sands at Broadstairs to pee. The feel and the smell of that wet sand is still in my nostrils 66 years later, and I think I felt that same sense of shame then as I would now if I were to pee in my pants.

MIRIAM KARLIN

Beverley Sisters

Until we were evacuated in the war
we three had always slept in same
bed (with the twins on each side of Joy)

Our earliest memory is of mum finding
the bed very wet on one side and,
as Babs now admits, letting Teddie get the
blame.   Babs now says "I knew very
well it was me, I clearly remember the
lovely warm feeling of doing it!"

Beverley Sisters

From: Mrs EDWINA CURRIE MP

HOUSE OF COMMONS
LONDON, SW1A 0AA

20.3.96

I can't remember my earliest memory .... but I do recall the Coronation in 1953, when I was 6½ years old. It fascinated me. I kept an enormous scrapbook into which I placed newspaper cuttings & articles, and "scraps" - which were coloured bits of paper, pictures of the State Coach and the horses and the Lord Chamberlain: & most of all, the Queen.....

Edwina

NATIONAL VIEWERS' AND LISTENERS' ASSOCIATION

ARDLEIGH, COLCHESTER, ESSEX CO7 7RH.
Tel: Colchester (0206) 230123

PRESIDENT:
MRS MARY WHITEHOUSE, CBE

GENERAL SECRETARY:
Mr John C. Beyer

HON. CHAIRMAN:
Rev. Graham Stevens

14ᵗʰ March 1994

As a very little girl I attended the Column School at Shrewsbury, an infant school which I believe has long ceased to exist. I only have one memory of my very short time there - it is of being scolded for climbing on the desk instead of sitting and behaving myself like a good little girl - well, that's what I remember the teacher telling me anyway!

Mary Whitehouse
President.
National Viewers and Listeners Association.

Jenny Pitman Racing Ltd.

FIRST MEMORIES OF THE FAMOUS

Riding my pony which was being led by
my father. We were rounding up his cows
prior to milking them.

Jenny Pitman.

Mrs J Pitman

Essex County Cricket Club

County Ground, New Writtle Street, Chelmsford, CM2 0PG
Telephone Chelmsford (01245) 252420
Fax (01245) 491607
Secretary/General Manager Peter J. Edwards

21 - 4 - 96

Dear Jill,

One of my earliest recollections is that when ever I was out with my parents walking along the street, I was forever "Turning my arm over" ie Bowling a Cricket ball — playing a straight drive with an imaginary bat. I must have scored quite a few runs + taking a fair number of wickets in my minds eye even at that early age of six or seven.

I remember my parents were always chiding me over this habit I had, although it turned out in later years I did manage to score a few runs. Hoping this will help.

Yours Sincerely

PETULA CLARK

One of my earliest memories is of sliding
down the coal tips on a tin tray in the
mountains of South Wales where I used to
stay with my grandparents when the London
air-raids became too dangerous.

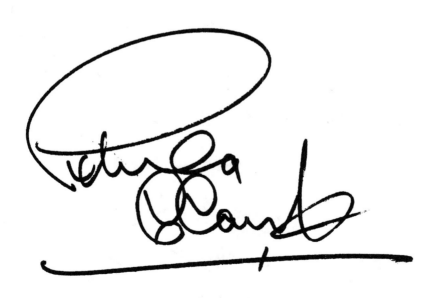

RICHARD WILSON

One of my earliest memories
is all _of us_ sheltering under my parents
bed during a bombing raid - we
hadn't been able to get to the shelter
in time. Frightening but, exciting
too!   Richard Wilson

HOUSE OF COMMONS
LONDON SW1A 0AA

My earliest memory is of the celebrations on V E Night which marked the end of World War II in 1945. I was three at the time and can clearly recall the fireworks display and the general festivities in my home town in South Wales.

With best wishes

Neil Kinnock

From: Joanna Trollope

A sunny afternoon in, I suppose, 1945, when I would have been about eighteen months. I'm sitting on the carpet, very fatly, (which I was) and it's brown, except where the sun strikes it, where it's yellow. There is a ring of adults standing round me, peering down, and I am very conscious of their faces, and their eyes. Their eyes are all fixed on something I am holding which I have been given by a kind American airman. I don't know what this thing is because I have never seen one before — I just know that they all want it, long for it. It is my first banana.

Joanna Trollope

BILL OWEN M.B.E.

c/O BBC TV CENTRE
lONDON W12 7RJ

25th January, 1994

Dear Jill Bernhardi,

My contribution as follows:

I was a wee boy between three and four years of age and my 'big day'
had come. The South Acton Wesleyan Methodist Sunday School annual
outing – my first. We went by char-a-banc to Burnham Beeches; in those
far-off days, deep into the countryside of Buckinghamshire. We had
stopped at a picnic site which also boasted a small Fair, a donkey ride,
a coconut shie, a roundabout and a hurdy-gurdy,which groaned forth a
popular song of the day. This setting of the scene was gathered from my
mother during my later childhood. But my first memory and only one of
that day, was being lifted down from the char-a-banc, then hand clutched by
my Sunday School teacher, as I stood refusing to budge, fascinated by the
man who was turning the hand-wheel of the hurdy gurdy.

Then there was that tune, still crystal clear, it's still with me, I
whistle it but no one can tell me the title! As forthe lyric, all I
know is the last line – "....... Nelly Kelly, I love you". Any answers?

Yours sincerely,

DAVID ESSEX
Queen's Theatre

Nov 17th 93

My first Childhood memory was a trip to
Battersea Fun Fair around the time of the Queen's
Coronation. I remember a giant plastic figure
of a giant and losing my Cubs hat on the
Water Shute

David Essex

Sir Bernard Ingham

April 7, 1996.

Dear Mr Bernhardi,

"I can't work out my earliest memory, though walking
in procession through Hebden Bridge at the Coronation
of King George VI in 1937 is one of them. I was then
four. But one early memory is for ever printed on my
mind. I was walking alone down the hillside terrace
where we lived to visit my grandparents' home ten or so
doors below. The valley was filled with an old-fashioned
peasouper. Suddenly, out of the fog and over the ash
tree at the bottom of the terrace roared a bi-'plane.
It was obviously lost. A few minutes later it flew
into the hillside across the valley. I must have been
one of the last to catch a glimpse of the forlorn
pilot alive. From that moment on, I was terrified of
low flying aircraft. I did not get over it until well
into the war which brought lots of air traffic over
even that safe, hidden backwater called Hebden Bridge."

Bernard Ingham

25th March 1996

Dear Jill Bernhardi

Thank you for your letter of the 15th March. My earliest memory is of throwing my toy railway engine in a rage at my cousin Bob Boothby on the lawn of my grandfather's house at Nairn in Scotland during one summer holiday. I had expected to be chastised for this. What I had not expected was Bob Boothby (then a rising MP) doing a <u>quid pro quo</u> and throwing it back, narrowly missing me. I think I was three at the time.

Yours sincerely

(signature)

(Sir Ludovic Kennedy)

FIRST MEMORIES: WINSTON S. CHURCHILL MP

"Let's Have a Crash"

Among my very first memories when I was just three years of age at the height of the Second World War is of my Grandfather - who had certain other responsibilities to occupy him at the time - laying his hands upon a second-hand clockwork model railway set, not the easiest thing to come by in war-time London.

When it eventually arrived he seemed as excited as I, getting down on his hands and knees to help assemble the circular track. To his delight there were two locomotives in the set. With a gleam of mischief in his eye, he declared: "Winston, you wind up one engine, I'll wind up this one and we'll put them back to back. Let's have a crash!"

Winston Churchill

28 February 1996

From: KEITH VAZ MP

HOUSE OF COMMONS
LONDON SW1A 0AA

Dear Jill

My earliest memory is when I was two and half years old, we visited Nairobi. We visited the circus during our holiday and when we returned home I remember giving a blow by blow account of all that had happened. The adults were beside themselves with laughter by my accuracy and that only encouraged me to go on. I also remember giving sermons because my ambition was to join the priesthood and then on to becoming Pope!

With all good wishes, for all the hard work that is done by the MacMillan service,

Yours sincerely,

KEITH VAZ

Memory plays odd tricks, I know, but I think I remember a carnival going down Binley Road in Coventry where I lived as a child, and my father lifting me up so that I could see it pass by. My first 'theatrical' experience!

Nigel Hawthorne.

My first concert performance was at a very early age for a working men's club. My sister Sylvia, brother Alec and I were an act - not a very good act, but we were cute. Our moment in the concert finished the first half. Our routine had been worked out so that Sylvia was to go on first to grab the audience with her dynamic acrobatics. I would come on halfway through to knock them out with my song, while Sylvia still cavorted behind me. Then Alec, the baby, would steal their hearts with his drumming. As we were all babies really, nothing could happen for certain. That first time, Sylvia, being the most responsible and intelligent of the three, did her thing professionally, then gave me a nod to come on, but I didn't move. Either I had stage fright or I didn't feel like it - but whatever the reason I wasn't going on, and all the cajoling backstage couldn't make me budge. As Sylvia came to the end of her routine she got exasperated with me, and walking to the side of the stage grabbed me and dragged me on. It did the trick. I stood on my given mark and sang my little heart out. Once there, they could not remove me from centre stage. I loved it! I even loved the ridiculous song that had been assigned to me - 'Let's all sing the barmaid song'. Strange words coming from a frumpy three-year-old with fuzzy hair and a big red bow on top of it all! But I was not to be removed. I absolutely enjoyed being the centre of attraction, so much so that the silly song was sung over and over again. Eventually Sylvia came to the rescue, breaking off a high kick to push me to one side, away from my limelight, to allow Alec to start his awful drumming. The audience by this time must have been in hysterics at our goings on. Eventually Sylvia managed to shuffle us into line, persuaded us to bow, and then shoving, pushing and pinching us in the direction of the exit cleared the stage for the interval.

"I remember walking through rows of sweet peas on my grandfather's allotment while he held my hand. I must have been about 18 months old, and wore baggy bloomers. He wore a black waistcoat and trousers and a walrus moustache. He had blackberries scrambling over brass bedsteads, and a tumbledown shed full of old gardening tools and seeds. It was on the banks of the River Wharfe in Yorkshire, and I can see it now as clear as day."

from Alan Titchmarsh

Ashburnham
SW 10.

Dear Mrs Bernard(i)

1st memory

About 2½/3 at
High Ham Somerset - picking
Buttercups with an Aunt
Getting bored I said "perhaps
we'd better leave some for
Some one else's mummy"
Not sure if I remember
it or if I've been told
it so many times!

Ne[...] Sher[...]

Jill Bernardi

Be prope[...]
[...]
post[...]

FROM DIANA RIGG Aged about 4,

I remember lying in bed,
recenting being in bed,
watching the yellow bed-room
curtains billowing in the
breeze, and then nothing
— I must have fallen asleep!
    Diana Rigg